5 Keys

to building a
clear & **usable**
website

Gwen Davies

5 Keys to building a clear & usable website

Design: Kathy Kaulbach, Touchstone Design House

Bright Crow Publishing
Halifax, Nova Scotia

ISBN: 9 781522 916475

Contents

Start to build a working relationship by using plain language

Steven Pinker studies language. He says, "Language comes so naturally to us that we're apt to forget what a strange and miraculous gift it is." He also says, "[C]hildren have no instinctive tendency to write but have to learn it through instruction and schooling."

There is the problem in a nutshell. We talk naturally. Writing is something we have to learn. Using something we have to learn often makes us self-conscious. What we write sits there on the page where others can see and judge it.

Writing also gives us more opportunity to manipulate what a reader takes away, as you will see in a minute.

This short guide helps us write more naturally, closer to the way we talk. Using the techniques and guidelines of plain language, we go back to what drives us to speak, which is to communicate simply, directly, and clearly: Pass the bread. That will be $29.95. Are you ready? Because this book is about creating clear websites, we focus **on** ways to help people understand what we write and take action.

No one who bought this book would write the sign in this example:

"If you headed to the [Florida] Gold Coast this holiday season, there's a chance you came across some signs warning you of the 'potential for dangerous aquatic organisms' in the canals. This actually means you should watch out for the bull sharks rather than some kind of microbe attack. Luckily, the sign includes a (very small) picture."

– *The Drum*, Neil James. mobile.abc.net.au/news/2014-12-31/james-worst-words-of-2014/5994446

The sign manipulates language to take care of a legal obligation while trying to NOT say what it means. However, even when we set out to be clear, we may use language — and design — that is almost as baffling as that sign. Why? Usually it is because we do NOT think about the person who is trying to use our writing to take some action. We have only thought about writing.

Here is an idea to start with: Communicating with one another is about creating a relationship. A website is a working relationship. My intention is to give tools to make your website into a place where people can see what to do and can do it easily. Like developing a good serve in tennis, getting good at this stuff takes some work. And it is so satisfying when you get it.

Welcome to the international conversation on plain language. It goes by many names, works in many languages, and also goes under the banner of clear communication. The kernel of communicating clearly is this: as a writer, we need to know how our readers use, read, and process information. However happy you feel about what you write, writing is NOT plain, or clear, if the reader does not understand it. The job of making communication work is yours, as the writer.

On line, a website sets up a conversation. Though many plain language principles are the same for communicating in print and on line, there are differences. This book gives you the basics about communication that works online.

A thought to take with you

The person coming to your site wants to take some action. **Use these t**hings **to** help them do that

- Design a website to play an equal role with the words in giving your message.
- Use as few words as possible, and use the words of the people who come to your site.
- Keep the main site simple and link people to further information.

To give someone a longer piece to read

- link them to the longer piece – an essay, instructions, regulations
- summarize the piece in a thumbnail – a few lines from the piece or a short summary
- tell them what format the piece uses – pdf, ms word, etc.– and how long it takes to read

Time now to have a little conversation.

For awhile, we referred to people coming to use a website as "users." This reminded us that they came to take action, not sit and read. However, more recently it seems important to have empathy, which is easier to have for a "person" than a "user." This book goes with terms like "people" and "audience" and sometimes even "reader," depending on what is appropriate.

What makes clear communication such a challenge

We use our own words when we write. Buried in those words are whole processes that we know and other people don't, and understandings that we share with others in our field.

A government department of environment has a page called "Fact Sheet for Homeowners."

This is how the page begins

Homeowner/Occupant Responsibilities
Once a spill has occurred the homeowner or occupant responsibilities include, but are not limited to, the following actions:

First, the text seems to pick up in the middle of a conversation. There is nothing to give you a framework.

The top item on the menu bar to the left is "Contaminated Sites." If you click on it, you will find the beginning of the conversation. It is the second paragraph:

Spills and chemical releases can occur over time undetected. They can also occur as a result of immediate events such as oil tank leaks aboveground. When this happens, soil, water and air can become contaminated.

The writer uses the word "spill." As a word, it is easy to read. However, it means something specific here because it is used as a term. That term, when used for homeowners, usually refers to home heating oil that has spilled from an oil tank or fuel line.

The writer also says, "include, but are not limited to," adding a legal clause where it is not necessary.

We often assume that other people know what we are talking about, which means we leave the background out, particularly when we use terms, jargon, and acronyms.

To write for someone who does NOT know the context, you need to think about what you write from the other person's side.

What you know the most about, you are the least good at explaining.

What this book does

- It gives you tools including strategies, check lists, tips, examples, and references.
- It helps you figure out exactly what you need and want your site to do.
- It lets you
  - assess how your site visitors think and speak
  - build an easy-to-use, clear website
  - make sure people can use your site quickly and successfully

Most strategies in this guide work for any site, from a one-page, check-out-my-salon site to the national site of a large organization. I will let you know when a process makes more sense for larger organizations only.

Who will find this book useful

- You **if you** are starting a small business and you want people to find you.
- **You when** everyone says you need a website **but y**ou do NOT have a clear idea of what you need it to do or how to make it useful.
- You **if you** work at a non-profit where too much staff time goes to answering the same simple questions over and over, by email and by phone.
- You **if you** have a website that looks OK but you feel like it could do more. Like what?

Why this book is useful

Using plain language helps you do these things

- be clear about what you want
- create a website that does what you want it to do
- save time
- save money
- make life so much easier for people who come to use your website

Saving time and money

"An average business wastes as much as 40% of its managing costs because of poor communication."
– William H. DuBay. *Working with Plain Language*. Costa Mesa, California: Impact Information, 2008.

"When FedEx revised its ground operation manual into plain language, users found information they needed more easily. The changes saved the company $400,000."
– Joseph Kimble. *Writing for Dollars, Writing to Please*. Durham, North Carolina: Carolina Academic Press, 2012.

CHECK LIST: **The easy-to-use website**

- ☐ Remember that you are an expert and many people who come to your site are not.
    - ☐ Make the information clear for anyone coming to the ideas for the first time.
    - ☐ Explain terms. Spell out acronyms the first time you use them.
- ☐ Use the language people coming to your site use.
- ☐ Let people scan. The fewer words you can use to make sense, the faster people can find what they want and do what they came to do.
- ☐ Organize your website to flow logically from task to task.
- ☐ Design your website to look clean and feel easy to use.
- ☐ Design your website to show what is most important.
- ☐ Design your website to show people how to work through it.
- ☐ Make sure people can see themselves in any pictures you use.
- ☐ Use a little humour when it helps to make your point.
    - ☐ Make sure your humour helps, and does NOT confuse or get in the way.

There IS a magic bullet for making your website work: test your site.

Testing is the Fifth Key

- Running a test is simple and quick.
- Testing makes your site useful and reliable.
- A useful and reliable site saves you money and time.

5 Keys to Building a Clear & Usable Website

1

Plan Your Site to Make It Work

Planning is an unnatural process; it is much more fun to do something. The nicest thing about not planning is that failure comes as a complete surprise, rather than being preceded by a period of worry and depression.
– Sir John Harvey, 1863-1944 British Actor-Manager

Save time by planning your website. Here are two planning strategies to help you do that.

STRATEGY 1: **Get your purpose clear**

STRATEGY 2: **Think like someone using your site when you write**

In the book, we will use this case study to help clarify steps in building a website.

CASE STUDY

I want to create a website for my business. People have told me that I can't run it without one.

The business is renting and selling costumes. I run three small stores **in three small cities.**

Get your purpose clear

You do any job long enough and there's some degree of tunnel vision. You can't assume your reader has the same background context and knowledge as you. – Whatcom County Council member Rud Browne

Think you already know what you want to do? (I'm selling a service; it's pretty clear to me.) Maybe, but can other people see what that purpose is when they come to your site?

Break your purpose down

What elements are involved in putting together a website? How do they all work together?

Start with what you know

Do you find websites that frustrate you, talk down, or seem to withhold the information you need?

EXAMPLE

You fill out a form, click all the boxes, and when you hit "send" you get a message that says you forgot to click what city you're in. Nowhere can you find a place to show what city you're in. You click the "back" arrow. All the information you entered is gone.

No one sets out to make a website to frustrate you. It takes some planning to create a website that is clear and easy to use.

For starters, "clear and easy to use" means different things to different people. This section helps you figure out what "clear and easy to use" means on your website.

Before you work with the check lists, take a look at how brainstorms and mind mapping can help you **bring your plan to life.**

Brainstorms and mind maps are good tools for getting at ALL your ideas.

HOW TO

Using a brainstorm gives you a more useful list of people to work with.

Maybe you want everyone to look at your website. But – what about aiming it at those who will buy what you sell or use your service? Or people who have trouble using it?

This takes about 10 minutes. Tape a large piece of paper onto a wall. Gather some coloured markers.

Start playing with ideas about who might come to your site. Picture all kinds of people. Write down odd ideas and every idea.

Go away and do something else.

Come back and choose who you want to create your web site for.

HOW TO

Using a **mind map** gives you both a list and a chance to explore the list further.

"In a mind map, as opposed to traditional note taking or a linear text, information is structured in a way that resembles much more closely how your brain actually works."

litemind.com/what-is-mind-mapping

To help you create a mind map, tape paper onto a wall so that you have a large sheet to work on, and gather together a few coloured marker pens.

Once you know your purpose, you are half way to planning your site.

Use these questions and check lists to START your brainstorm or mind map.

FIRST QUESTION: **What will a website do for you?**

CHECK LIST: **The working website**

☐ Tell people where you are, what you do, and how to get in touch.

☐ Tell people what your business does and does NOT do.

☐ Sell things.

☐ Ask for donations.

☐ Start a national dialogue about an issue.

☐ Make resources available.

☐ Update public services.

☐ List regulations.

☐ Help users follow a set of rules.

How much time do you want to spend looking after your website once you put it up?

CHECK LIST: **The maintenance plan**

☐ Update it. How often?

☐ Write a blog

    ☐ What would a blog add to what you want your website to do?

    ☐ How often (be realistic) will you have something new to post on that blog? (Hint: It helps to set a regular time to post if you want to do this.)

    ☐ Will you read the blogs of the people who come to your blog?

☐ Create a forum to let users give you feedback.

    ☐ What will you do with the feedback you get?

    ☐ Will you monitor the forum or not?
    (Hint: Some feedback can be abusive.)

☐ Create a site that you leave alone and let it speak for itself.

The answers to these questions help you decide on the purpose of your website.

✳ A **blog** brings more users to your site because search engines look for sites that have new material on them regularly. Here is a simple definition of a blog
www.youtube.com/watch?v=Oiov0L4bIIw

Find navigation tools

Navigation tools include menu bars, and, for a larger site, a site plan* and a good search engine. Navigation tools guide people through your site.

Good menu bars let people find what they're looking for. We will look more at that in the **Third Key** under _Make sure your menu bars work._

If you have a larger site, you need to create a site plan, and use a search engine on your site.

* **Site plan**: a plan, like a map, that lists all the things you deal with on your site and shows where they are. Users do not see it. Your menu bars, your links, and your search engine help you figure out your site plan. Here is a simple definition along with some straightforward directions. wordtracker.com/academy/learn-seo/technical-guides/how-to-create-sitemap

Think like someone using your site when you write

If you're trying to persuade people to do something, or buy something, it seems to me you should use their language.
– David Ogilvy

Use this check list to assess what you know and what you need to know about the people who will use your website.

CHECK LIST: **Profile of a person coming to use your site**

☐ How much time does this person have when they come to your site?

    ☐ Can they do what they need to do in a few minutes?

    ☐ If not, will they quickly see that the site is easy to work with? An easy site will bring them back.

☐ What screen are they using at this moment?

    ☐ Are they on a tablet, computer, cell? How will your website work on each type of screen?

    ☐ Will they be using older equipment?

☐ Are you stating the obvious? People come with life experience. Most of them will feel annoyed if you talk down to them. People who are annoyed may NOT come back.

☐ What background do you have that this person may NOT know?

    ☐ Find ways to identify and include background that people need. Particularly be careful with jargon and acronyms.* Remember that some people will speak English as a second (or third) language.

* **Acronym**: a word or set of letters created from the first letters of the main words in a name or phrase: SEO is the acronym for search engine optimization.

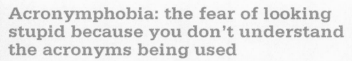

Acronymphobia: the fear of looking stupid because you don't understand the acronyms being used

Test your language. Find out what works for people who use your site.

SOLUTIONS

- Use acronyms ONLY if they will appear several times on your site.
- Spell out the name or phrase the first time you use it and put the acronym after it, in parentheses: search engine optimization (SEO). Do that most of the time.
- Put the acronym first, the first time you use it, IF the acronym is what most people will know. Spell out the name AFTER the acronym, in parentheses: SEO (search engine optimization).
- Use capital letters for all words, such as DOH instead of DoH for the Department of Health.
- Make a list, if you need to use a lot of acronyms, of the acronyms and what they stand for. Link the acronyms to the list.

BEFORE AND AFTER

This sentence works for some people and NOT for others.

BEFORE The state DFW called on the BPA to conduct a DEIS to ensure that BAS is used when assessing the impact of LWD in EFH.

AFTER The state Department of Fish and Wildlife called on the Bonneville Power Administration to conduct a draft environmental impact statement to ensure that best available science is used when assessing the impact of large wood debris in essential fish habitat.

What language you use depends on the AUDIENCE. If your site is for engineers, use clear language and enjoy the jargon and acronyms. Do remember that for some people, English is not their first language.

Example adapted from an article by Dean Kahn, *The Bellingham Herald*, July 26, 2014

Now it is time to look closely at who is going to use your website.

Create user profiles of people who will use your site

There are three steps in this process.

First, figure out all of the people you want to attract to your site.

Once you know who you want, you can figure out what language they will use.

At the same time, you can also start to understand how these people will use your site.

Creating these profiles is also called "persona development."

Start by generating a list of all the types of people you want to come to your site. You may want to use a brainstorm or mind map to do this.

Coloured pens and large sheets of paper taped on the wall are useful here.

The process you use depends on the type of list you want.

From my research, I decide that I want these people to come to my site

- groups who put on themed events, large and small
- adults and children at Hallowe'en
- friends going to a party
- people who like to use costumes for any and every reason
- all types of performers

Next, look for patterns in the types of people.

To look for patterns, group all the users on your list into two or three categories.

For my costume stores, I will divide the people who I want to come to my site into three categories: buyers, renters, and job seekers. Keep it simple.

Finally, create a persona or user profile for each category.

Creating a user profile helps you imagine actual people and begin to work with them.

- Make a quick sketch of one face on one piece of paper. I'll start with "buyers." This sketch will be my representative buyer.
- Give your profile a nickname. The nickname reminds you of what that this person wants to do on your website. My buyer is Generous Aunt Jay. I'll call the renter Sam the Student and the job seeker Hungry Bubba.
- Start labelling your profile.
  These labels will help me understand Generous Aunt Jay. First, I decide she is in her late 30s, she buys unusual and imaginative presents, she has a stable income but is not wealthy, and she lives in Hong Kong. She likes my stock but likely goes to other sites, she gets me to mail gifts directly to her niece and nephew in Gibraltar, she usually orders gifts while on public transit, and **she** uses a tablet as her main screen. She speaks English as a third language.

- Generate lots of labels for each user profile – you could even use a mind map for this. Think about things like these: age, how the person is feeling when they come to your site, whether they do this type of task often or are new to it, and how distracted they might be. The more you know, the better your site will serve the people who come to it.

SECOND KEY

Write Your Site to Serve Your Visitors

The biggest problem with communication is the illusion that it has been accomplished. – George Bernard Shaw

I have worked with plain language for 30-some years. This second key is the heart of the work I have done, and where I give you my favourite writing strategies.

STRATEGY 1: **Use language to build a relationship**

STRATEGY 2: **Use only the words you need**

STRATEGY 1:
Use language to build a relationship

Write the way you talk – to someone running out the door.

Get out your user profiles. Which profile represents the people you most want your site to work for?

Start talking. Out loud, tell them each thing you need them to know. Write down what you say. This trick will give you a good tone to use to write your first draft.

Before you start writing your first draft, consider using a brainstorm or mind map to decide what you want to include on your site.

Once you know what you want to include, consider finding an organizing principle that will help you put your content in an order that flows easily from one topic to another.

Write your draft.

The two things to focus on while you write are who you are talking to, and what you want them to know. Get that down. Edit it once you have it written. Send the thought police out for coffee while you do this. This is a draft, NOT the final copy.

When the draft is down, you begin to shape it. That is what this section is about. Even the most-experienced writers edit their drafts.

First, cut the draft down to the bones. You'll get better at this with practice. Edit a piece of writing, put it away for a day or two, and work with it again. Each time you do this, you get better at cutting what you don't need and making sense of what you keep. It is a life lesson.

Next, look at all the people you are writing for and imagine how people on that list will use your site. Are some parts more important to one profile group and others parts to others? You DO need your site to be consistent – to sound as if it all comes from the same person or organization. However, you may need to aim different pages at different people.

For my costume stores, I will design specific information each of these

- everyone who wants a costume
- people who want to buy costumes
- people who want to rent costumes
- people who might be a little off the beaten path who want costumes
- people who want to work at one of the stores

Work on your overall draft first. Then, have an intimate talk with each group about what is important to them.

Test your next-to-final draft. It's worth it to make sure your site works.

Use language that is clear to the people you are writing for

When you read, you ilter text through your experiences and past conversations. You put words into context. You interpret.
– Jason Santa Maria

Look for the language that is most familiar to your audience.

You may need to do a little research.

EXAMPLE

This example comes from information sheets on vaccines. Both give the same basic information, but they give it to two different groups. Notice how different the wording is for each.

For parents, the writing assumes the person has no background; for health-care professionals, the writing assumes the person knows the background and terms.

FOR PARENTS

Mothers are often the ones who look after new babies. You can protect your baby by getting a vaccine as soon as possible after the baby is born.

Fathers and anyone who takes care of the baby can get a vaccine before the baby is born. The whooping cough vaccine is free for adults in Nova Scotia.

FOR HEALTH-CARE PROFESSIONALS

Vaccines are the best way to prevent mortality and significant morbidity from pertussis. We need to make sure that infants and young children follow the recommended schedule, and that their caregivers and close contacts have been immunized recently.

Make the message accurate.

This web page tells people from outside the country how to apply for a professional licence. The "before" example softens the message, but that makes it less accurate. It also uses language that is overly complex.

BEFORE AND AFTER

BEFORE Applicants who graduated from non-accredited programs may be required to write technical exams to confirm their knowledge in various areas and demonstrate that they are academically qualified.

AFTER If you are a widget maker who is educated outside the country, you must write the National Professional Exam (NPE) in order to apply to register with the local Association. You may also have to write the National Technical Exams (NTE).

This "before" example uses jargon and buzz words that are vague. Different readers may define these words in different ways.

BEFORE We make a positive contribution by providing our members with responsive, value-added programs and services.

AFTER We support our members, respond to their needs, and offer them programs and services they identify as useful.

Make the message specific.

Show your user exactly what they need to know. Separate the information from the sales pitch. People using your site know the difference.

BEFORE AND AFTER

These examples use vague words. Vague words do NOT sell. They annoy.

BEFORE The online tool is meeting the HR needs of nearly any kind of employer.

AFTER This gives employers an online tool they can use to find business advice.

BEFORE This is a job best left to a professional cleaner who has the training and experience in doing this in a safe manner.

AFTER Sewage spills are dangerous. Hire a professional cleaner who has the training and equipment to clean up a spill safely.

BEFORE Individuals and organizations wishing to apply must file applications with the appropriate offices in a timely manner.

AFTER You must apply at least 30 days before you need the certification.

   a. If you are an individual, apply at the State office in the State where you reside.

   b. If you are an organization, apply at the State office in the State where your headquarters is located.

– from plainlanguage.gov

If the people coming to your site share a common language, you can use it too. This example comes from a plain language booklet for judges, police, and lawyers. The words are clear and familiar to the people who work in these professions. It includes some jargon.*

There is also provision for the youth justice court to review prohibition orders that are made under s.51.

* **Jargon**: Special words or expressions that are used by a particular profession or group and are difficult for others to understand. (Online Dictionary)

Jargon is not the same as a term of art. A term of art is "a word or phrase that has a specific or precise meaning within a given discipline or field and might have a different meaning in common usage." (Dictionary.com)

You may use jargon on a site for people who all work for the same company or department, or who work in the same field. However, keep these three things in mind

- People may have different definitions of the same word.
- Some people will be new at the job and not know the jargon yet.
- Some who speak English as a second language may never learn the jargon.

Take a look back at the section on *Write the way you talk.*

Use only the words you need

Simplify your words, sentences, and paragraphs

Writing improves in direct ratio to the things we can keep out of it that shouldn't be there. – William Zinsser

"Simplify" is not a general term. It refers to the simplest words that work for the people you want to talk to.

Simplify your words.

First, choose the simpler word unless you have a darned good reason for choosing the more-complex one. People are skimming your site, not reading it.

Next, use the same word for the same thing all the way through your site. Every synonym* makes people stop and wonder if this means the same thing as the word you used earlier. Save synonyms for writing your novel.

* **Synonym**: A word that has the same meaning, or almost the same meaning, as another word: begin/start, utilize/use, impact/effect.

BEFORE AND AFTER

Choose the simple word.

BEFORE The program commences . . .
AFTER The program starts . . .

BEFORE Retain this receipt . . .
AFTER Keep this receipt . . .

("Retain" doesn't actually make sense. "Keep" is the accurate word.)

BEFORE A studio rental agreement will be issued specifying details of booking.

AFTER We will send you a rental agreement that includes booking details for the studio.

Making it clear sometimes takes longer.

BEFORE Our Work Diary tracks time and takes work-in-progress snapshots, giving you visibility into project progress and accurately tracking time spent.

AFTER Our Work Diary tracks time and takes snapshots of the employee's work as they do it. You watch the project progress and track the time the employee spends.

Check out the handy *Convoluted Terminology* section (see page 77) of complex to simple words.

Simplify your sentences.

TIP **As you simplify your sentences, pay attention to your tone.** Keep in mind the people from the user profiles. If you were talking to them, would they get upset if you used the same tone as you're using to write to them?

Two things that annoy people who are trying to get a job done

- writers who try to sound important
- writers who clutter the page with things readers don't need (even if those things are clever and witty)

Start with what is familiar.

BEFORE AND AFTER

BEFORE Our Law Firm provides notarization services at a cost of approx. $30 (dependent on the number of documents, how many pages, and on them being fully completed).

AFTER We notarize documents. The minimum cost is $30. The final price is based on the number of documents, the number of pages, and how much information you have already filled in.

Make your point as directly as possible.

BEFORE As your account specialist, you will have direct access to me so that I may assist you with all your business needs.

AFTER I will be your account specialist. Please contact me when you need help.

This example also confuses information and "sell."

BEFORE We offer a variety of international retail hair products and styling tools to maintain your look.

AFTER We can sell you the same shampoos and styling tools that we use.

Keep sentences short.

BEFORE As per Section X, "Review and reporting on registration practices in the Act," a public report will be produced to reflect the procedural fairness, objectivity, transparency and impartiality of the regulatory body's registration practices.

AFTER Section X of the ABC Act outlines what regulatory bodies need to focus on as they create registration practices that are objective, transparent, impartial, and procedurally fair.

TIP A lot of commas in a sentence usually show that you need to break the sentence up. Check this site on why we need short sentences insidegovuk.blog.gov.uk/2014/08/04/sentence-length-why-25-words-is-our-limit

Simplify your paragraphs.

Put the most important information first. Again, watch your tone.

BEFORE Research studies show that while most children can adapt to the parents' separation, ongoing conflict has a strong negative impact on children's development and relationships, and on their outcomes as adults.

AFTER Research about parents who separate shows that most children can adapt to the parents' separation. It is the ongoing conflict between parents that harms them. Ongoing conflict continues to get in the way as children grow and develop, form relationships, and become adults.

Sometimes you need more words to replace jargon and make your message clear.The bullet point in this sentence is one of several in a longer list. The point twists around. Use active verbs. (Keep going. They come along two pages down). Take the time to say what you mean simply and directly.

BEFORE We have the following goals:

- improve accessibility to the Adult Learning Program within the province and ensure that the learning achieved is recognized and transferable among programs and provinces

AFTER We have these goals:

- to make sure that what people learn is recognized and can be transferred from program to program and province to province

Don't be afraid to use an informal tone if it suits your message and those who read it.

Tumbl'r Terms of Service / Privacy Policy / Community Guidelines

BEFORE AND AFTER

BEFORE No individual under the age of thirteen (13) may use the Services, provide any personal information to Tumblr, or otherwise submit personal information through the Services (including, for example, a name, address, telephone number, or email address). You may only use the Services if you can form a binding contract with Tumblr and are not legally prohibited from using the Services.

AFTER You have to be at least 13 years old to use Tumblr. We're serious: it's a hard rule, based on U.S. federal and state legislation. "But I'm, like, 12.9 years old!" you plead. Nope, sorry. If you're younger than 13, don't use Tumblr. Ask your parents for a Playstation 4, or try books.

From *Business Insider* www.businessinsider.com/tumblrs-new-terms-of-service-is-inspiring-and-funny-2014-1

Let words do the work they do best

Speak properly, and in as few words as you can, but always plainly; for the end of speech is not ostentation, but to be understood. – William Penn

Language and actions are connected in the brain. Verbs . . . tend to stimulate the brain to take action, especially if they're active verbs. – Your *Brain and Business: The Neuroscience of Great Leaders*, Dr. Srinivasan S. Pillay

Get your verbs* working.

Verbs give you the action of a sentence.

* What's a verb?

The action in your sentence happens in a verb.

These verbs are called "active" verbs. You can tell an active verb most of the time because whoever (or whatever) does the action comes right before the verb.

> **Click** on the button . . .
> You **can manage** your own file . . .
> The company **will use** . . .
> We **had provided** . . .

The "to be" family are also verbs – "is, are, was, were, will be." They often work with other verbs to let you talk about the past or the future

> The contest **was running** . . .
> You **will see** a copy of the photo . . .

Use more active verbs.

Active verbs are usually the best verbs to use. Active verbs help people take action. Taking action is what you want people who come to your site to do. Use a lot of active verbs.

> **Go** to . . . **Fill** in . . . **Read** this before . . .

When you talk directly to someone, the verb you use is automatically an active verb.

> **Complete** the form.
> **Check** your passport details. **Make sure** they are correct.
> **Buy** one and **get** the second at cost.

(The subject of these sentences, the person you want to take the action, is "you." We do NOT include the subject in this type of sentence. A grammar book would say that the subject is "understood.")

Active verbs give you active sentences. When you use them, you are using the "active voice."

EXAMPLE

Here is how an active sentence works.

> **We use** only fresh, local **ingredients**.

It starts with the **subject** – a person or thing > We (subject)
Next, it adds the **action** the subject takes > use (verb)
Then, it adds the **object** that receives the action > ingredients. (object)

You can then add the other words that you want to use. In this sentence, you add "only fresh, local" to give the full meaning of what you want to say. These words are modifiers. We don't need to spend a lot of time on modifiers in this book.

Here are the subject, verb, and object parts of a couple more active sentences

> This page gives you information . . .
> You will find a full range of products . . .

Choose when to use passive verbs.

There are other kinds of verbs called passive verbs. Passive verbs give you passive sentences. Passive sentences also have their uses.

Passive sentences generally put the receiver of the action first. The verb comes next. Some passive sentences include the subject. In passive sentences, the subject comes after the verb. Also, some passive sentences leave the subject out.

Passive verbs need a few support words to make them work. Check out these examples.

EXAMPLE

Here is an active sentence.

Our dieticians support our clients.

subject or actor > dieticians
verb or action > support
object or receiver > clients

Here is the same sentence using the passive.

Our clients are supported by our dieticians.

To make the sentence passive, we added two words. One before the verb or action > are
One after the verb or action > by

If you use the word "by" and then add the actor, you have a passive sentence.

We could also write the sentence like this.

Our clients are supported.

Here are three types of sentences where a passive verb is useful

- when the action and the receiver of the action are important but the subject is NOT

  If your payment is returned for any reason . . .
  Your membership will be processed by the next business day.

(Note: The word "by" is used in this sentence, but the words that follow it do not include the actor. The "next business day" is not going to process your membership. The sentence does not include the person who will do that.)

- when you have no reason to talk about the actor

  Everyone is encouraged to get a flu shot.
  Effective safeguards can be provided.

- when no one takes responsibility for an action

  The Thursday clinic is cancelled.
  Your appeal has been denied.

These three examples show sentences where a passive verb is NOT useful.

We tend to think that passive verbs sound more professional. Are we confusing professional with writing that is merely impersonal?

It is harder to take action when directions use passive verbs.
PASSIVE A receipt can be generated by clicking here.
ACTIVE Click here to generate a receipt.

Passive verbs can confuse people and leave them feeling uneasy.
PASSIVE Your concerns will be addressed by the property manager.
PASSIVE Your concerns will be addressed.
ACTIVE The property manager will address (talk to you about) your concerns.

Passive verbs can intimidate people.
PASSIVE Registration must be completed before the commencement of the term.
ACTIVE You must register before the term starts.

Avoid making verbs into nouns* or nominalizations.

Stay calm, we can make this easy. Nominalizations are a wonderful way to confuse a message.

✳ What is a noun?

Nouns are things, pretty much: gift, purchase, hair cut, appointment, receipt.

Nominalizations are words that started out as action words — verbs — and got made into things — nouns. The actions were "nominalized" which is why some people call these types of nouns "nominalizations."

Nominalizations often go together with passive verbs. Like passives, they also need extra words to make them work.

EXAMPLES

It is harder to take action when the directions use a nominalization.
NOMINALIZATION WITH PASSIVE Payment can be made directly by credit card.
ACTIVE You can pay by credit card.

The extra words you need with a nominalization can slow a sentence down.
NOMINALIZATION Upon completion of the installation . . .
ACTIVE Once you install . . . Once we have installed . . . When we finish installing . . .

Nominalizations with passive verbs can confuse a simple process.
NOMINALIZATION WITH PASSIVE Flag Stop – Requires Boarding Passes to be purchased 24 hrs. in advance to guarantee passenger pickup.
ACTIVE Flag Stop – You must buy a Boarding Pass 24 hrs. before your bus leaves to make sure the bus stops at your Flag Stop.

Nominalizations with passive verbs complicate simple information.

NOMINALIZATION WITH PASSIVE Value is extremely dependent on condition and many stamps have been intentionally altered to "look" better and these take experience to identify.

ACTIVE A stamp's worth depends on its condition. Many stamps have been altered to "look" better and you need experience to identify what is an original stamp.

Avoid jamming too many words together into noun strings.

We often jam words together to create a term or a name: *Obesity Monitoring and Weight Loss Management Clinic*

We think that our string of words says everything we want to say. However, these strings are usually hard to understand. When people do not understand, the words say nothing.

Strings of words are hard to break apart. However, there are solutions.

BEFORE AND AFTER

BEFORE We offer community-based vocational day programs.

AFTER You can take vocational programs during the day in your own community.

When you create a term using a string of nouns, you also assume that people who read them know a lot of background information. For the term in the example above, you probably should define "vocational programs," or use an example to show what they are.

If an official name of an organization is a noun string, like the one in the next example, you are stuck with it even if it is hard to understand. One way to cope is to make it clear by its context – the information that comes before and after it.

BEFORE PEN is an on-line source of scientifically sound evidence-based information about food, nutrition and dietetic practice. Subscription to Practice-based Evidence in Nutrition (PEN) is included in our membership.

AFTER PEN (Practice-based Evidence in Nutrition) is an online source of information about food, nutrition, and dietetic practice. We base our information on scientific evidence.

Many names that are made up of noun strings are too long to use over and over. Many users have no idea what the initials mean, even when they are acronyms for popular terms like SEO (Search Engine Optimization).

As the PEN example shows, you can use an acronym and include the full term after it, in parentheses. OR you can use the name followed by the acronym in parentheses.

If there is a single word in the name that works, such as the word "Justice" in the name "The Santiago Department of Justice," you can adopt that word to refer to the organization rather than using an acronym.

9:00 Wed morning. I turn on my computer and this is what I do

- Delete 15 emails I don't need.
- Scan seven emails to see what they are about and put them into folders for the future. (Except I probably will not come back to them in the future.)
- Star four emails to remind myself to deal with them later.
- Delete several starred emails that I have not dealt with and the deadline has passed. Oops.
- Read seven important or really interesting emails.

Why did I choose those seven emails to read right now?

I looked at who sent them and what the subject line said. The subject line tells you what the email is about. Most of them were also short. If one of them was long, I probably read the first two paragraphs, scanned it, and maybe starred it for later. Later usually looks like right now, however: I am busy and distracted.

Write good subject lines.

Think about two things when you write a subject line

- What makes you read an email as soon as you get it.
- What context you can give the receiver. Giving context tells the receiver what is coming, and lets them find the email again later.

Use these strategies to write good subject lines

- Make them specific.
- Let the receiver know if they can deal with the email quickly.
- Use key words and put them first to help the receiver find the email later.
- Make the subject line interesting. Hook the reader by asking or answering a question, for example.

Examples of good subject lines.

- Meet on Sept 24 or Oct 29?
- Deadline June 18 for final report and final billing
- Edit 3 Jan 12, 2014 Chapter 6 Small Business and Diversity
- Proposal and cost estimate for catering the reception March 8
- Bio on the workshop leader for First Aid for Non-Profit Boards
- Two quick questions about the space heater
- For your reference: gallery guidelines and hours

Get your emails read.

Before you write, answer two questions

- Does the person really need this email? (Would this person agree with you if you think they need the email?)
- Would a phone call work better to take care of this?

Here is a website that tells you when the telephone makes more sense.
"The Phone Lady proves that telephone communication still outranks texting and email in the business world."
thephonelady.com

Problem

You send three emails, with good subject lines, with all the information that receivers need for a meeting. Several people show up knowing one thing and nothing else. Or they write just before the meeting and ask for the info you already sent.

Solutions

Think about what makes YOU read through an entire email. Use the following quick check lists to guide your writing.

Keep it short.
CHECK LIST: **Quick and easy emails**

- ☐ Leave out what the person already knows.
- ☐ Use key words with very little in between. Give the receiver only what they need to know.
- ☐ Break the email up with headings.
- ☐ Use point-form lists.
- ☐ Put the most-important info first. Write the rest in the order of most important to least important – the inverted pyramid.
- ☐ Leave out what you WANT to say, and include only what you NEED to say.

Think about the receiver as you write.
CHECK LIST: **The context of an email**

- ☐ Include key words in the subject line to give some context. Put key words first.
- ☐ Send the information in the order that is useful for the receiver.
- ☐ Is the receiver in a rush? If so, give them the fewest number of words you can.
- ☐ Is the receiver distracted by a work demand? Give them a really clear subject line as reference so that they can find the email later.
- ☐ Is the reader using a hand-held device? Keep the email as short as possible, use key words, and write a good subject line.

Sometimes you are the one in a rush. Practice making the first email work. It is faster than having to write another email to clarify the first. Take an extra half minute to clear your mind and another one to read the email over before you send it. Read it out loud.

CHECK LIST: **Good email protocol**

- ☐ Write as if you were having a conversation.
  - ☐ Picture the receiver getting the email.
- ☐ Tell the receiver the basics about any attachments.
  - ☐ Note the format. Say what is in the attachment. For example, include the name, date, time, and place of an event in your email. A receiver may NOT open the attachment.
- ☐ Use the simplest format possible. Formatting often does NOT transfer from one email program to another.
  - ☐ If you need to format something, use the formatting from the email program rather than importing it from your word processing program.
- ☐ Include a signature with your name and contact info.
  - ☐ Use a simple type face for this. The goal is to make it easy to read.
- ☐ Check for typos and unclear wording.
  - ☐ That way, you don't have to write another email to explain what you meant in the first one.
- ☐ Give sensitive emails a little time before you send them.
  - ☐ Re-read them. If anything seems bothersome, listen to your instinct and wait. Clear your mind and read it again. Read it out loud. Imagine receiving it. Ask someone else to look it over.

Organize Your Site to Flow

3

Organizing information makes it easier for you to express your ideas clearly, and it is critical to ensuring that the reader stays with us. Readers . . . don't tolerate disorganization because they don't have the patience. – Ken O'Quinn

These two strategies will help make your site easier to move through

STRATEGY 1:   **Organize the text**

STRATEGY 2:   **Let people move into your site and around it easily**

STRATEGY 1:
Organize the text

Find a useful order for all the bits and pieces

Find an organizing principle that gives your whole site a sense of moving logically. Which logic you use is less important than having a logical order. Two things to remember

• Make the organizing principle obvious.

• Use an order that makes sense for the material.

Organize the pages on your site to match the overall logic of the site. Make them easy to move through.

Back in the First Key you created a plan. Now it is time to create an order for the elements of your plan. What goes where on your site? What goes on each page?

To organize the elements, write each one on a sticky note or a small piece of paper and move the pieces around. Play with these until you find an order that works.

For a smaller site, the menu bars give you the main destinations on your site.

For a larger site, you need a site map.

As you map out where things go, think of your home page as the starting place – the front lobby. Do this even though not everyone will start at your home page.

Use your home page to introduce yourself. Use it to tie everything on your site together. Make it interesting and brief. Most of all, make it useful.

Organize a smaller site.

Look at other sites that are about the same size as yours.

EXAMPLE

Here is a small site that is organized around a simple menu bar www.andreaprzygonski.com.au. Each page comes directly from its own single menu item. The menu bar is the same on each page.

This page belongs to a visual artist. It is lovely to have art to put on the site but you can also box important text, use good quotes, and add a graphic that reinforces your message to make any page interesting and still easy to use.

For example, if you have a hairdressing shop or a small pottery studio, you might have a 'GALLERY' page to show pictures of your work, an 'ABOUT US' page to give your hours, background, and training, and a 'CONTACT' page to give your address, phone number, and email address.

Users will want to know these things
- where you are
- when you are open
- what you DO and do NOT DO
- who the site is for – who you serve
- who to contact for what

What is the difference between using a menu or navigation bar and using a site map?

"Navigation bars provide a consistent method of moving throughout a website one page at a time. Typically, a navigation bar will allow you to move forward and back. It might also have links to the home page and other important elements of the website. Often a link to a sitemap will be included on the navigation bar. A sitemap link gives the user quick access to all areas of the website, making it easy to jump from section to section."

from 21cif.com/tutorials/micro/mm/sitemap

Map a larger site.

Your plan from the First Key is also the best place to start to create a site map.*

＊ What is a site map?

It lists all the main elements that are on a site, and it shows how all those elements relate to each other. It can be a list, or a visual map, like what you find at the main entrance to a shopping mall or on the wall of a subway station. A site map can also give an overview of a larger organization.

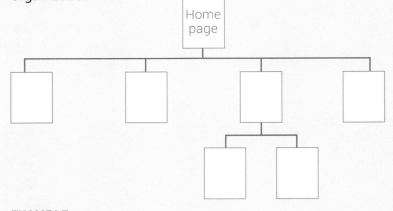

EXAMPLE

This page gives you several examples of site maps and how they work www.smartdraw.com

On a large site, use your home page to lead people to "pathway pages." A pathway page gives people links to the contents of your site. It works just like the table of contents in a book.

EXAMPLE

This is the pathway page you get when you click on "Topics" on the home page of Nova Scotia Environment. It links every topic the department wants to tell you about www.novascotia.ca/nse/topics.asp

These pathways, and the pages they lead to, are all set up on the site map.

The search engine on a large website, and search engines (and spiders and crawlers and bots) on the web, use key words to connect to your site map. Make it easier to connect the way you list things on your site map, and what the search engines search for. That will make it easier for visitors to find what they are looking for.

Organize within the site

One of the most useful ways to organize information is the inverted pyramid. Start with the most-important information and end with the least important. Journalists almost always use this organizing principle.

To use this style, you start with the most-important information, or the conclusion. Next, put the second-most important information. Carry on until you finish with the least important information.

HOW TO

Here is a useful discussion about using the inverted pyramid in writing for the web. "By front-loading your web content, you are more likely to keep your readers on the page." webwisewording.com/inverted-pyramid

Here are some other ways to organize information

- Cluster like things together.
- Follow the order in which things happen – chronological order.
- Give general information first and then give specifics.
- Give answers and then give reasons.

And a few more

- Use questions & answers or frequently asked questions – Q&A or FAQ.
- Follow a process step by step.
- Start with what people know and lead them to what is new.
- Use an "If . . . then . . ." format.

Break up the text

Use a lot of headings.

"Wallpaper" is the term for a page with a lot of unbroken text on it. People don't know where to look. Finding information looks overwhelming. What to do?

First, get rid of as many words as you can. People scan on line. Meet them half way and make your text as short and simple as possible. If you want to write something longer, give it a page and link to it.

Headings break the text up. They also give the framework of what you are writing, let people scan to see if they have found what they're looking for, and attract the attention of search engines and spiders.

Headings do these jobs
• create an informal table of contents
• give people an efficient way to scan the content

• break text into short chunks that people can grasp

quickly **Use key words in headings.**

This example from Jakob Nielsen shows two things
• how key words work in online headings
• how and why online headings are different from print headlines

EXAMPLE

Print headlines are different from online headings.

HEADLINE: **Coping With the Tall Traveler's Curse**

"The headline lacks key words — such as 'airline seat' and 'hotel bed' — that are important for search engine optimization (SEO). No one will search 'curse' when trying to find out which hotel chains offer extra-long beds or which airline seats are the least unpleasant for long-legged travelers."

An online heading would include "tall traveler," a specific or key word a tall person would search for.

Jakob Nielsen "Writing Stye for Print vs. Web"
www.useit.com/alertbox/print-vs-online-content.html

Keep headings short.

The magic number is 65 characters in one heading, including spaces, says the UK government. Use colons to break up longer headings. Put key words first.

BEFORE AND AFTER

BEFORE How to create and when to use achievement-based objectives

AFTER Achievement-based objectives: how to create them; when to use them

Make headings specific.

BEFORE AND AFTER

These show general, vague headings in the before and specific headings in the after.

BEFORE Participation opportunities
AFTER Develop personal skills by working in the community

BEFORE Introduction
AFTER Why we chose to study rural architecture of PEI

BEFORE The project
AFTER How we conducted the project

BEFORE Submission of applications
AFTER How to apply or How to submit your application

Use questions and answers

If you use questions and answers, or FAQs (frequently asked questions), make sure you use questions that someone would actually ask.

EXAMPLES

Is there a rain location [for the festival]?

Why do I have to register?

Do you help graduates find internships?

What types of therapies do you offer?

Where can I write the exam?

What happens after I file for an appeal?

Use lists

Another way to break up text is to use lists. Lists also help you simplify complex information. Here are more reasons to use a list

- to show several steps people need to take
- to separate the elements of complex information
- to deal with a lot of information that you want to keep together

HOW TO

How to set up a list.

- Introduce the list with a full thought whenever you can.
- Start each point with the same kind of word: noun (a thing), verb (an action), or another part of speech.
- Get out of the way by using as little punctuation as possible.
- Break up long lists (more than 5 points) by clustering things that belong together.
- Include only the information you need.
- Make sure everything in the list belongs in the list.

Lists set out steps in a process.

You can number steps in a process. You can also use bullet points, as this example. You follow the steps in this list in order.

EXAMPLES

To develop your own plan of action, be realistic:

- confirm your overall objectives
- decide which area you wish to work on
- list one or two tasks that you wish to undertake to achieve your goals
- identify how much time and resources are needed to do each task
- decide who will do each task

– from Co-operative Housing Federation of Canada – Diversity Action Kit (pilot)

Lists separate the elements of complex information.

Again, break complex information into small chunks to make it easier to grasp.

BEFORE AND AFTER

BEFORE We are recognized internationally for our adult education and facilitation training and programming related to transformational learning and spiritual deepening.

AFTER Here's what brings people to us from all over the world

- We train adult educators and facilitators.
- Our programs offer you transformational learning and spiritual deepening.

Lists let you keep a lot of information together.

This shows people, visually, that all of these elements are part of one process or idea, and breaks them into small chunks to make them easier to read.

BEFORE AND AFTER

BEFORE Relationships Australia provides a quality specialist sexual concerns counselling service to individuals and couples who wish to address any of the following concerns: differences in levels of sexual desire, loss of sexual desire, painful intercourse, inability to achieve orgasm, erection difficulties or sexual functioning that has been affected by chronic illness, surgery, disability, the ageing process, child sexual abuse, or general issues about sexuality. The service also provides opportunities for sexual enhancement through learning new ideas and techniques.

AFTER Relationships Australia provides sexual counselling to individuals and couples. Our specialists can work with you on any of these

- personal issues
  - differences in levels of sexual desire
  - loss of sexual desire
  - painful intercourse
  - inability to achieve orgasm
  - erection difficulties
- effects of outside factors
  - chronic illness
  - surgery
  - disability
  - ageing
  - child sexual abuse

We also work with general issues about sexuality, and help you learn new ideas and techniques to help you enjoy your sexual relationships more.

Let people move into your site and around it easily

Get a good search engine

Search engines are computer programs that search documents for key words. A good search engine can find many more things than even an almost-good search engine can. Use a search engine for a large website.

You can use Google Search, one of the best search engines, on your website. *Government sites should use this search engine.*

HOW TO

Check out how you can get Google Search on your website at www.digitaltrends.com/web/how-to-make-google-your-default-search-engine

Getting search engines to find information on your site is called search engine optimization, or SEO. Check out this guide for everything you need to know about SEO.

"There are many aspects to SEO, from the words on your page to the way other sites link to you on the web. Sometimes SEO is simply a matter of making sure your site is structured in a way that search engines understand."

moz.com/beginners-guide-to-seo

There are also spiders, web crawlers, or bots* on the web that are busy searching through information. This definition comes from the web.

* "A **spider** is a program that visits Websites and reads

their pages and other information in order to create entries for a search engine index. The major search engines on the Web all have such a program, which is also known as a **"crawler"** or a **"bot."** Spiders are typically programmed to visit sites that have been submitted by their owners as new or updated. Entire sites or specific pages can be selectively visited and indexed. Spiders are called spiders because they usually visit many sites in parallel at the same time, their
"legs" spanning a large area of the "web." Spiders can crawl through a site's pages in several ways. One way is to follow all the hypertext links in each page until all the pages have been read."

whatis.techtarget.com/definition/spider

Make sure your menu bars work

Menu bars use key words. Key words are the simplest, most-specific words you can find to sum up the main bits and pieces on your website: Buy clothing from India, Gift cards, Upgrade, Donate, Support school lunches.

Users generally read only the first word or two of an item in your menu bar.

Design your menu bars.

Your goal in putting together a menu bar is to let people find what they want. These are a few design ideas. See more on design in the Fourth Key.

HOW TO

- Use good contrast between the words and the background.
  - You can find free sites that tell you what colours contrast well and look good together. Even for users who are colour blind.
- Use large enough type that most users can read it easily.
- Decide how many menu bars you actually need.
- Put all menu bars where people can find them quickly.

On a larger site, use drop-down menus. They keep the page simple and help users find what they want. Organize the items on a drop-down menu to make sense in two ways

- in relation to the items they come before and after on the list
- in relation to the item they drop down from

Keep drop-down lists short.

It is OK to make menu items interesting, but do NOT
sacrifice meaning to be clever.

EXAMPLE

Here is an interesting drop-down menu under the main
menu item "Travel Extras" at the site of Maritime Marlin
Travel www.maritimetravel.ca

Travel extras
   emergency travel service
   travel tips
   staff picks
   inside scoops
   travel insurance
   destination services

TRAVEL EXTRAS
EMERGENCY TRAVEL SERVICE
TRAVEL TIPS
STAFF PICKS
INSIDE SCOOPS
TRAVEL INSURANCE
DESTINATION SERVICES

CHECK LIST: **Useful menu bars**

☐ How many menu bars do you need on a page? There
   are plenty of answers to questions like this one on
   line. Check this out https://blog.kissmetrics.com/
   common-website-navigation-mistakes/

☐ Do you have a good reason, if you repeat menu bars?
   This site says we should stop using menu bars for
   larger sites. Almost. http://www.webdesignerdepot.
   com/2014/01/3-reasons-we-should-stop-using-
   navigation-bars/

☐ Do you know where people look for menu bars? Hint:
   They look here, in this order: left, top, and bottom.
   Most users do NOT look for menu bars on the right
   side of the page.

What style of menu bars make a site easy for you to use? Do an informal test – ask your friends what works for them. Ask them about drop-down menus.

Does this work for people who come to your site? All drop-down menus drop down together here www.sfu.ca

This site for the University of Barcelona sits on the site for International Students Abroad. It uses different menu bars for different types of users studiesabroad.com/barcelona?gclid=cjgkeajwkpacbrcnlpr ww-u-nbwsjacwhiw--rx0kmxahjbj9ur2kiieeaxtwq9ho4yrhtu 4ojs_7vd_bwe

TIP

Use key words from your menu bars in your headings.

Test your menu bars.

Organizing information to make it flow well is as important as writing clearly and designing to make the page look easy to use.

4

Design Your Site to Make Your Message Clear

Content precedes design. Design in the absence of content is not design, it's decoration. – Jeffrey Zeldman

I would add that the most-effective process is to develop content and design together.

STRATEGY 1:   **Show people your business**

STRATEGY 2:   **Make your site accessible**

Use design to make your communication clear.

- Show people who you are and how you do business.
- Let people see at a glance what is important and how to use your site.
- Reinforce what your page says and make your information accessible.
- Let people see how to do what they want to do.

Show people your business

As you work with design, remember that good design accommodates a text reader for people with visual impairment.

CHECK LIST: **Plain language design**

☐ Make your website look like the other materials that represent you: brochures, posters, ads, business cards.

☐ Match the feel of the site to the type of work you do or service you offer.

☐ Make sure the technology does NOT drive the site. (The content should drive the site.)

☐ Let the user move easily through the site. (Test it to make sure.)

☐ Leave your site free from things that move or make noise. (A user must click to hear or watch any music, moving images, or video.)

☐ Use a logic for each page to make it look clean and easy to navigate.

☐ Put the elements that a person is looking for where they expect to find them. Make them easy to find.

☐ Use headings to break the text into small chunks and guide people through through the content.

☐ Break menus and lists into small clusters.

☐ Give people what they expect when they click on a menu item. (Test it to make sure.)

☐ Take people to what they want in one or two clicks – or through a simple, clear process.

☐ Let the design show what is more important and what is less important.

- [ ] Make sure everything on a page works together to create a single impression.
- [ ] Make sure everything on a page is there because it serves a purpose.
- [ ] Make sure the whole website is consistent, and works together as a whole.
- [ ] Put the forms that people need to fill out right where they need them.
- [ ] Make sure you really need all the forms on the site.
- [ ] Keep your pages simple, and link to things like essays, videos, clusters of pictures, and other sites that give more information on a topic.
  - [ ] Give people a thumbnail that tells them what they will find when they click on the link to one of those essays, videos, etc.
  - [ ] Tell people what format they will find when they click on a link – particularly if the link goes to a pdf. (A pdf can take a long time to load on some systems.)

Decide how to approach the task of designing your website

Will you do this yourself? Will you hire someone? Will you hire two people: a web developer and a graphic designer?

First, go back to the plan you developed in the First Key and see what you want your site to do.

Second, decide what YOU can do and what you want help with.

Third, read through this section to find ways to design a website that is clear and easy to use.

Make your site consistent

When you hire a designer or a web developer – often a good thing to do – they will probably use a template. A template gives you a flexible, pre-set design for the style, formatting, tables, graphics, and other standard elements on a website.

Use templates if you are creating your own site. You can find good, free templates online, such as at www.freewebsitetemplates.com

Templates help you make good decisions and take steps like these

- think about your website as a whole, as well as each of the pages
- set up blocks of images and text so that they work together
- create a consistent website (users will find it easier to use)

HOW TO

Here are some ideas for finding the right template.

Look at sites you like and think about the layout – text here, image there, menus where you want them. Look for a template that sets the page up in a way that looks good to you. Make sure there is a place for each of the elements you want on the page. This takes a little practice for a complete novice. Ask friends and colleagues. Go to sites like this one for advice www.networksolutions.com/education/how-to-choose-web-design-templates

On a larger site, different people may develop and look after different pages. You need to make sure all of these people start with the same template and agree on some design principles. You may want to choose these together.

However it is put together, other people think of your website as one site. They will expect (and try) to use all parts of it the same way. A site with different approaches on different pages is frustrating to use.

A good template is flexible and it gives you a basic grid to work with. The grid lines up the elements on the page and shows how everything relates to everything else in that space. You need a grid.

Hire the help

A person's first visual impression of your website sets up how they will always see you and your business, your service, or your organization.

If they are successful finding what they want, they will always think of your business as one that is easy to work with.

You may want a web developer AND a designer. Developing the site and designing it are different processes. Not many people are good at both.

First, research the person you want to hire.

Hire a web developer.

Look at sites they have developed. Watch for these things

- the site works on a small device as well as a desk-top and laptop
- nothing moves (unless you click to make something move or start a video)
- nothing makes sounds (unless you click on something like a video or a piece of music)
- navigating the site follows a simple logic

If you have a LARGER site, you need to use a scalable design. Scalable design allows your website to change so that it is easy to read on different screens including tablets, lap tops, cell phones, glasses, watches . . .

If you have a SMALLER site, what you gain by creating a scalable site is NOT worth the expense.

Hire a graphic designer.

Consider these three things

- Check your designer's web work before you sign a contract. Some graphic designers are good at paper design and not so good at website design.
- Make sure everyone who works on your site is able to work together, and work with you, to make your vision happen.
- Look at sites they have designed. Watch for these things
  - You like how the sites look, for yourself and for your users.
  - The text stands out against the background to make it easy to read.
  - The type size is large enough for anyone to read, and not so large that it is out of proportion.
  - You can see at a glance what is important.
  - The fonts feel right for your tone and message.

HOW TO

The typeface you use is an important part of your design. This is still a fairly new field. "With the floodgates poised to open and the promise of many typefaces being freed up for use on websites, choosing the right face to complement a website's design will need to become another notch in the designer's belt. But where do we start?"

alistapart.com/article/on-web-typography

Do your research.

Talk to at least two clients of anyone you may want to hire. Ask about how well they did with things like these

- listened, collaborated, and in the end did what the client asked them to do
- helped the client understand the process
- fixed problems and misunderstandings quickly
- made a site that was easy for the client to change and keep up

Ten design tips that make your website a treat to use.

- The design shows people how to read the content.
- The images say visually what your words say.
- There are no background images behind your text.
- The text is dark enough to show up well against a light background. Unless there is a good reason to do something else.
- The typeface is sans serif and big enough for almost everyone to read. The style of it reflects what your website is about. Check out this site alistapart.com/article/on-web-typography
- The site avoids using more than a few words of italics and all capital letters. (Online, when you use all caps you are shouting.)
- Underlining is used for links only.
- There are no lines that stretch across the page. Some people will confuse these with page breaks.
- The page is laid out on a grid, where things line up, and where headings are flush left.
- Colours convey the right message for the cultures you serve.

Look at a few websites that have a similar purpose to yours. Study what works and what doesn't work. Use what you think works. Test it to make sure it works for other people.

www.thecreativeunderground.net

Make your site accessible

Here are some interesting online discussions about ways to present information.

HOW TO'S

Here are four HOW TO's that can make your website more accessible.

Replace tables with slopegraphs.

"Tables aren't inherently bad. But they are used too much in presentations, and have some problems.

Good – they're useful to look up actual numbers. They're very easy to cut and paste.

Bad – they're usually difficult to read, with small text. Column and row titles get shortened to acronyms to save space. And they sometimes contain numbers you don't want to talk about.

Here's one alternative to your table – the slopegraph." makeapowerfulpoint.com/slopegraphs

Create interactive text and images.

"'Show, don't tell' dictates the famous credo in creative writing. Maybe it should say: show and tell. Communication often benefits from the combination of text and images. Within one message, some meaning is best encoded using written language while other information is best expressed in a picture, a graph, a diagram or a map. Combinations of these representational modalities are part of all kinds of genres, like news reports, textbooks, scientific articles, advertisements, comics, and even novels."

www.basbroekhuizen.nl/2014/03/12/how-to-integrate-text-and-images-with-interactivity

Make a memorable infographic.

"[W]hen we do retrieve a memorable image, a surprising amount of information comes with it, like a burr stuck to a sweater. That insight could have big implications for people who use visualizations in their everyday lives--graphic designers, for instance, or anyone on Tumblr. Above all, it suggests that memorability alone might enhance an infographic's effectiveness. But it also prompts a question: How does an image become memorable in the first place?"

www.fastcodesign.com/3021394/evidence/the-secrets-of-a-memorable-infographic

Avoid giving users cognitive strain – a no-no.

Cognitive strain is what can happen when it is hard for a user to figure out what to do next. A user may lose confidence in the honesty of your site when they have to do things like read complicated instructions and look at text that is in **a** small font or has poor contrast with its background.

www.nngroup.com/articles/navigation-cognitive-strain

Bonus Section on Forms

When at last we are sure, You've been properly pilled,
Then a few paper forms, Must be properly f lled,
So that you and your heirs, May be properly billed.
– Dr. Seuss

Forms seem to be a fact of life on websites.

Users do not like them. They are afraid of them. They resist using them.

The definitive book on clear, useful forms is *Forms that Work: Designing Web Forms for Usability* by Caroline Jarrett and Gerry Gaffney.

The first rule of forms is – use them ONLY when you really truly NEED them. And when you need them, make sure they are easy to use.

The second rule is – make them work. To do that, look through this section, and then TEST the forms you create before you inflict them on the general public.

This is what people will do to punish you if you do NOT follow the rules

• make mistakes that will cost you time and money to correct
• make up information
• leave the site
• waste your time and theirs by calling or emailing to ask you how to fill in the form
• miss out on getting a service they need

Most of the information in this section is useful to any site that uses a form. Some of it applies more to larger sites. For more information, check the Resources section.

Think first

Think about what you want the form to do.
- Do you really need this form?
- Do you really need each piece of information you ask for in this form?
- Do users really need to register?

Note: In a larger organization, many people work on putting the website together. Ask each person who says they need a particular piece of information WHY they need EACH wpiece of "essential" information.

In *Forms that Work*, the authors tell us that forms have three layers

relationship – that you create between you and the other person

conversation – that you set up by the way you write the questions and instructions, and through the topics you deal with (see "cognitive strain" under Make Your Site Accessible above)

appearance – how you design the text, use colour, and arrange the areas where people give information

When you design a form, think about how YOU use each of those layers when you fill in a form.

You want people to fill in the form easily and, more importantly, correctly.

Think about what the other person wants

People want to get through the chore of filling in the form so that they can do what they came to do. You can help them by putting each form exactly where it is needed to do its job.

Use your user profiles to help you design forms. Every time you make a decision, run it by your profile gallery. Show your profile people what you are doing and see what they have to say. Talk to them out loud.

Accommodate people who have visual impairment. Are there other disabilities you also want to accommodate? Find out how to do that. There are websites to help.

If you have a competitor who makes it easier for people to get what you both offer, the research shows that your visitors will go to another site.

CHECK LIST: **Useful and rewarding forms**

- [ ] Give the form a professional look.
    - [ ] Design it on a grid. (You can find these online, no coding needed.)
    - [ ] Use your logo or your brand to show people who you are.
    - [ ] Make the form look clean, simple, and easy to use.

- [ ] Let people know what to expect from this form.
    - [ ] Tell them the purpose for each form you use.
    - [ ] List everything the person will need to fill out the form, including documents, verifications, and the
    - [ ] like. Show the person how to get help if they need it.

- [ ] Write the form in a logical order.
    - [ ] Show the person through the process as if you were going through it with them in person, step
    - [ ] by step. Give information first — and then sell, if selling is your business.
    - [ ] Give options whenever options are possible.
    - [ ] Include "other" as a category if you want the person to choose from a list of options.

- [ ] Break the content in the form into small chunks.
    - [ ] Put things together that belong together.
    - [ ] Use white space or headings to separate the chunks.

- [ ] Help people recover when they make mistakes.
    - [ ] Design the form to save correct information that the person has already entered.
    - [ ] Show the person where the mistake is.

- [ ] Use words the person will know before you introduce words and terms that may be unfamiliar.

- [ ] Let the person choose first and then act. Put tick boxes AFTER the question.

This form uses a question and answer format. Always put your question first.

Date: _____

Name: _____

Phone # (home):_____

Phone # (work):_____

Email (home): _____

Email (work): _____

City and postal code: _____

Workplace name: _____

There are many ways to discourage a person who is trying to fill out your form. Try to use NONE of them. Look at what makes forms work for you. Read information on making forms work. They are one of the causes of anxiety that we CAN avoid.

Never mind if your form is only four lines long. If it is frustrating, the person trying to use your site will feel less friendly toward you, and your goods and services. The next section, on testing, gives you several ways to check your forms to make sure they work.

Test Your Site to Make Sure It Works

Listen to people, to find out what they really want. For example, the team knew, from web statistics, that people want information about tax codes. Through conversations, they learned that people want to know one specific thing: 'Am I using the RIGHT tax code?' Ahhh! That's the type of detail you can learn from listening. – From the gov.UK team

Testing is listening. It is an essential step in creating plain language. Once you test, you know two things

- what people understand when they read your site versus what you thought you wrote
- what people want versus what you have given them

This key guides you through the basics of usability testing.

STRATEGY 1: **Figure out what to test**

STRATEGY 2: **Choose the right test and run it**

Figure out what to test

Using usability tests

What should you test?

Every aspect of your site: wording, design, organization, flow, menu bars, graphics, forms. You can test these things separately or together.

There are two times that it is most useful to test

- as you start to put your site together
  - Test pages as you go to make sure the most-important sections and pages work. Once you know they work, use them as your template for creating more.
- when you finish developing your website
  - Test the whole glorious site.

Testing tells you what confuses, misleads, or irritates people.

Testing tells you what lets people move through the site quickly and easily.

Most important: test while you are still willing to change whatever doesn't work.

HOW TO

You can run the tests in this book yourself. I have adapted them from the website of the US Federal Plain Language Guidelines at www.plainlanguage.gov/howto/ guidelinesFederalPLGuidelines/testing.cfm. Take a look at the original site if you want more information. There are many other websites that talk about testing.

You can also run a readability test on what you write. It gives you a grade level, but it won't tell you if the writing makes sense.

STRATEGY 2:

Choose the right test and run it

Here are several ways to test what you are doing with your website. This section gives you a "How to" on testing.

One-on-one usability testing

What you need to do.

- Test in person.
- Use 1 volunteer for each test.
- Run 3 tests.
- Allow 1 hour per test.
- Make 3 appointments at 1-hour intervals.

When to test.

- Run the first set of tests when you have a good draft or mock-up.
- Run a second test after you make changes from the results of the first test. This tells you if your changes solved the problems without introducing new ones.
- Run a third test after you make changes from the results of the second test. This tells you what really works.

Who to test.

Find three people to test your site each time. That means you need nine volunteers. Make sure they represent the range of people who should be able to use your site.

Can people follow the way you want them to move through the site? What instructions or pieces of information do people most need to understand? If your site includes any forms, make sure you test them.

How to set up a test.

- Decide what particular information you want from this test.
- Based on what you want to learn from the test, decide what parts of your site to test to give you that information. You can test processes. You can test language, design, how things are organized, forms, graphics – everything on your site.
- Let the volunteers know what processes and parts of the site you want them to work through. They are doing a role play, so ask them to imagine that they need to perform the task you give them.

How to run a test.

Do NOT explain, defend, or interpret the site to your test volunteers. Always step back and ask them to see if they can solve a problem. You learn what works and what does NOT work by watching and listening to your volunteers as they work with the site and the problems it presents.

1 Welcome the volunteers and introduce yourself. Help the volunteers feel comfortable by asking them a few questions like
   - what they look for when they go online
   - how comfortable they are with technology

   These types of questions also let you know what to expect from these volunteers.
2 If you are testing the whole website, ask volunteers what they expect to find at this site. Take notes.
3 Tell your volunteers that you are testing the website, not them. Let them know that every problem they pick up helps you to make a better site. Tell them that you also want to know what works well. Reassure them again that you are testing the site, not them.
4 Ask your volunteers to work out loud so that you can hear what they struggle with and what they find easy.

5 Listen carefully to what the volunteers say. Take notes on these things
  - what they find easy
  - what they struggle with
  - what they understand
  - what confuses them
  - where they have to stop and think or reread before they can take action

6 Ask volunteers to tell you where they would expect to find answers when they get confused. Ask them how they would try to solve problems. Your best test results come from seeing what problems volunteers have and whether or not they can solve them easily.

7 End the session by debriefing with the volunteers. You do this by asking neutral questions about the experience like these
  - Was this site generally useful?
  - Is it what you expected?
  - Do you have any suggestions?
  - Is there anything you found particularly difficult?
  - Is there anything you found particularly helpful?

Co-discovery usability testing

What you need to do.

- Test in person.
- Use 2 or a few volunteers for each test.
- Run 1 test at a time.
- Allow 1 hour per test.

Follow the same process as for one-on-one testing with this variation: ask two volunteers to go through the process or section together and talk back and forth about it as they go. You take notes.

Or

Ask a few volunteers to work independently. Then bring them together to talk about their experience as a group. Divide the time equally between working independently and talking as a group. This works best if you have one note taker watching and listening to each volunteer as they work independently.

You may find it helpful to have two people take notes when you bring everyone together (or record the session and have one note taker) because people may talk quickly.

Remote, moderated usability testing

Follow the same process. Use web-based tools that allow you to test volunteers online while you are present with them online.

There are also online companies that do user-testing of websites, such as usertesting.com and Mile 7 mile7.com.

Remote, unmoderated usability testing

What you need to do.

- Test online.
- Use 3 volunteers for each test.
- Run 3 tests.

Ask volunteers to go through the materials and mark them up online. Find web-based tools that allow you to do this, and to tabulate the results.

Comparative usability testing

Choose either in-person or online testing.

Test different versions of your site or form. Ask each volunteer to work with both versions. Alternate which version people start with.

Ongoing user feedback

Note: This applies more to the site of a larger organization.

Add a place to your site where people can ask questions and answer each other, such as an online forum. These people will bring a great deal of knowledge and experience to your site and they will let you know what does and does NOT work.

For this to work, you need to monitor the online forum regularly.

"As soon as two users ask the same question, you should beef up your site to answer it unattended: Build a page, fix the navigation model, or tune your search engine."
– From Philip and Alex's Guide to Web Publishing
philip.greenspun.com/panda

The simplest test of all

Ask someone to work through your site, or the most important parts, or the tricky parts of it. Ask them to make notes all over the copy as they go, and to give the notes to you.

Read everything you write out loud.

Here are a couple of particularly useful sites on testing.

Testing content

by Angela Colter, Issue 320

Thumbnail

"Whether the purpose of your site is to convince people to do something, to buy something, or simply to inform, testing only whether they can find information or complete transactions is a missed opportunity: Is the content appropriate for the audience? Can they read and understand what you've written? Angela Colter shows how to predict whether your content will work (without users) and test whether it does work (with users). While you can't test every sentence on your site, you don't need to. Focus on tasks that are critical to your users and your business. Learn how to test the content to find out if and where your site falls short." – From A List Apart
alistapart.com/**article/testing-content**

Testing almost everything

The URL below takes you to a starter kit on a US government site that includes testing everything from processes to scripts. While this testing is designed for US federal government documents, there is much that is useful for testing any website.
www.digitalgov.gov/resources/digitalgov-user-experience-program/digitalgov-user-experience-program-usability-starter-kit

End Note

These 5 Keys give you a good start on making your website clear and usable. You will teach yourself as you go.

Once you tie in to the network of people who work with plain language, you can find endless studies and strategies. There are international forums, and many groups and organizations around the world that are busy making information clear and accessible.

Good luck. I hope these notes and resources serve you well.

Convoluted Terminology (big words)

accelerate (speed up)

accomplish (do)

accompany (go with)

accordingly (so)

accumulate (gather)

accurate (correct, right)

additional (added, more, extra)

adequate (enough)

adjacent to (next to, beside)

advise (tell)

aggregate (total)

altercation (conflict, fight, dispute)

amicable (friendly)

anticipate (expect, look forward to)

apparent (clear, plain)

application (the use)

apprehension (fear, worry)

appropriate (proper)

approximately (about)

ascertain (find out, learn)

assimilate (absorb)

assistance (aid, help)

assuredly (surely)

at the present time (now)

attempt (try)

augment (add to, increase)

benefit (help)

by means of (by)

capability (ability)

close proximity (near)

commence (begin, start)

commencement (beginning, start)

commendation (praise)

commitment (promise, agreement)

compensation (pay)

concur (agree)

concerning (about, on)

conduct a study (study)

configuration (shape, form)

consequence (result)

consequently (therefore, so)

consolidate (combine)

construct (build)

constructive (helpful, useful)

contains (has)

contribute (give, add)

correspondence (letter, memo)

deferral (delay)

demonstrate (show)

desire (want, wish)

determine (find out, learn, set)

detrimental (harmful, damaging)

due to the fact that (because, since)

duly (leave it out)

employ (use)

encounter (meet)

endeavour (try)

equitable (fair)

equivalent (equal)

erroneous (wrong)

establish (set, prove, show)

excessive (too much)

exhibit (show)

expedite (help, speed up)

explicit (plain, specific)

fabricate (make, build)

facilitate (ease, help, guide)

frequently (often)

herewith (below, here)

illustrate (show)

implement (do, start)

in order that (so, to)

in some instances (sometimes)

in the event that (if)

in close proximity (close to, beside)

in addition to (also)

inadvisable (unwise, stupid)

inaugurate (start, begin)

indicate (suggest, prove)
initial (first)
initiate (start)
in advance of (before)
in order to (to)
in relation to (about, with, to)
insofar as (because)
instigate (start)
interface (meet, work with)
in the amount of (for)
it is functional (it works)
locality (place)
maintain (keep)
materialize (appear)
maximum quantity (most)
minimum quantity (least)
modification (change)
modify (change)
necessity (need)
negatively impact (harm, hurt)
notwithstanding (in spite of, still)
numerous (many)
observe (see)
obtain (get)
operates (runs)
opportunity (chance)
optimum (best)
originate (start, develop, invent)
paramount (greatest, top, main)
past experience (experience)
perform (do)
permit (let)
pertaining to (about, of, on)
possess (have, own)
previously (before)
primarily (mainly)
prior to (before)
probability (chance)
proceed (go)
procure (get, buy)
proficiency (skill)
proliferate (spread)

provided that (if...)
purchase (buy)
pursuant to (in, under)
rationale (reasons)
regarding (about)
reimburse (pay)
remain (stay)
remuneration (pay, payment)
represents (is)
reproduction (copy)
request (ask)
significant (large, great
simultaneously (at the same time)
solicit (ask for, request)
submit (give, send)
subsequent (next, later)
substantial (large, great)
substantiate (prove)
sufficient (enough)
supersede (replace)
terminated (ended)
termination (end)
therefore (so)
time period (either one)
transmit (send)
ultimate (final, last)
uncertainty (doubt)
utilization (use)
utilize (use)
variation (change, difference)
verification (proof, check, confirmation)
visualize (imagine, picture, see)
with regard to (about, concerning)

©Joanne Wise, Wise Gillap
Editorials. Used with permission

The history of plain language

A paper that looks at democratizing language and the roots of plain language as a movement, by Sally McBeth http://www.en.copian.ca/library/research/plain2/index.htm#smcbeth

"When people demand proof that plain language works, we can now utter four short words: 'Read Joe Kimble's book.' Proof aside, it will also give them sound guidelines for creating clear documents, plus a fresh and inspiring history of our field." Martin Cutts, author of *The Oxford Guide to Plain English*

Kimble, Joseph, *Writing for Dollars, Writing to Please: The Case for Plain Language in Business, Government, and Law*. Carolina Academic Press, Durham NC, 2012.

Guides and online training

Particularly useful for government, with much information for anyone

Volunteers in the US government created and maintain a full, online training manual for plain language www.plainlanguage.gov

For everyone – a full training course

The UK government guides you through using plain language in a government context www.gov.uk/design-principles/style-guide

For plain language and health

This site offers free online training in plain language for people involved in health – and there is a certificate available. (There are few places where you can get a certificate in plain language.) https://plainlanguage.nih.gov/CBTs/Plainlanguage/login.asp

Guides to online design for particular audiences

To make your site accessible

"Sarah and Whitney present accessibility so that everyone can understand the core concepts of web accessibility, even if they have limited programming experience. Every web developer who is just starting to get involved with web accessibility should purchase this book!"
—Jonathan Lazar, Harvard University, Towson University
rosenfeldmedia.com/books/a-web-for-everyone/

For kids

Debra Levin Gelman explores how to design effective registration forms for kids based on their context, technical skills, and cognitive capabilities.
alistapart.com/article/designing-web-registration-forms-for-kids

Tests to see if your site works

Simple, low-cost usability tests to make sure your website works, and to find out what is most important to fix and how to fix it
Krug, Steve. *Rocket Surgery Made Easy*, New Riders, DK-8000 Aarhus C., Denmark, 2009.

Readability tests

Readability formulas analyse your writing to tell you its grade level. These give you one assessment tool, but it is only useful if you combine it with others. These formulas do NOT tell you if the words make sense
www.readabilityformulas.com/free-readability-formula-assessment.php

This simple test gives you the grade level of text and highlights particular problems
www.cynthiasays.com/Pages/Terms.aspx

www.hemingwayapp.com

Creating and using web sites

These three sites are well used in the IT industry

A List Apart alistapart.com/

Philip and Alex's Guide to Web Publishing by Philip Greenspun
philip.greenspun.com/panda

Alertbox on *Useit.com* www.useit.com/alertbox

Keeping your site visible

blog.scoop.it

Plain language guides

A complete how-to on plain language, with a piece on writing for the web
Federal Plain Language Guidelines, The Plain Language Action and Information Network (PLAIN) USA, rev. May 2011
plainlanguage.gov or go straight to the index
www.plainlanguage.gov/index.cfm

A look at how plain language can help a company avoid legal nightmares
drivingvalue.com/2014/09/26/plain-language-to-the-rescue

International forums on plain language

An excellent forum **started** by Cheryl Stevens, a veteran Canadian plain language specialist, on LinkedIn — search Plain Language Advocates Group

Clarity International is an organization that hosts international conferences and puts out a regular magazine on plain language www.clarity-international.net

Excellent speaker and writer about how clear communication works
Steven Pinker stevenpinker.com

Books on plain language

Thorough, useful, filled with practical examples from web pages everywhere

Redish, Janice, *Letting Go of the Words: Writing Web Content that Works* (Interactive Technologies). Morgan Kaufman, Burlington, Massachusetts, 2007.

Excellent. If you create forms, this gives you what you need to know

Jarrett, Caroline and Gerry Gaffney, *Forms that Work: Designing Web Forms for Usability*. Morgan Kaufman,Burlington, Massachusetts 2009.

A source of many books

Western Michigan University Cooley Law School is creating a plain-language archive of print materials. The archive is housed in a special-collections room that researchers will be able to visit and use. We will make the list of titles available electronically, and we hope to make them available by library loan. Link to the titles so far tinyurl.com/pjl463s (Posted fall 2014.)

Style and reference guides in English

www.fernwoodpublishing.ca

www.economist.com/styleguide/introduction

www.gov.ns.ca/cns/pubs/CNS-Editorial-Style-Guide-April2007.pdf

My primary sources – many thanks

Federal Plain Language Guidelines, Plainlanguage.gov, The Plain Language Action and Information Network (PLAIN) USA, revised May 2011

Clear Fresh Writing: A workshop for Nova Scotia Power Inc. Gwen Davies and Joanne Wise, 2010

Some useful plain language ideas and techniques

People are people, not users

Gerry McGovern says that empathy is an essential skill for those who design and manage websites and apps. It's hard to have empathy for a user

www.gerrymcgovern.com/new-thinking/people-are-people-not-users

Using jargon

"Even for specialized audiences it's still best to write as simple as possible. Even highly educated people don't want to struggle to read your site. You do not impress anybody by spouting highfalutin words or complex sentence structures that require careful parsing. People don't pay close attention to web content." – Jakob Nielsen

www.nngroup.com/articles/specialized-words-specialized-audience

"Jargon is not just overenthusiastic use of a thesaurus, nor is it merely harmless pretension. Jargon actually makes it harder for your brain to process information, which is why jargonists use it, it makes what they have to say sound more significant than it actually is." – Andrew Walker, Editor at Solar 350 Ltd.

www.linkedin.com/pulse/20140912083657-3265790-the-rise-of-the-jargonist-or-how-to-leverage-toss

Dealing with multiple languages

Video of the Plain Language Awards for the European Commission. Information on policy, legislation, administration, and Masters studies in clear communication. Attention to dealing with multiple languages. Just under 3 hours. You must create an account to use this site

www.linkedin.com/redirect?url=https%3A%2F%2Fscic%2Eec%2Eeuropa%2Eeu%2Fstreaming%2Findex%2Ephp%3Fes%3D2%26sessionno%3D7cdace91c487558e27ce54df7cdb299c&urlhash=dqZD&_t=tracking_anet

Gender neutrality

"Gender neutrality is important when writing about people because it is more accurate — not to mention respectful . . ."
www.justice.gc.ca/eng/rp-pr/csj-sjc/legis-redact/legistics/p1p15.html

Everything you ever wanted to know about singular "they"

"We gave up on the distinction between singular 'thou' and plural 'you' centuries ago, and it hasn't done us any harm. This means the so-called logical objection to singular 'they' is wrong.

In fact, logic is a poor guide to English pronouns, which are an inconsistent mess . . ."
stroppyeditor.wordpress.com/2015/04/21/everything-you-ever-wanted-to-know-about-singular-they

Using a graph

"Once you've built a draft of your chart, the next step in creating an impactful visualization is making sure all of its elements are labeled appropriately. The text components of a graph give your reader visual clues that help your data tell a story and should allow your graph to stand alone, outside of any supporting narrative."
infoactive.co/data-design/ch14.html

A Plain Language Thesaurus For Health Communications

"This thesaurus offers plain language equivalents to medical terms, phrases, and references that we often use. The technical terms found in health information can be confusing. This thesaurus is a tool to help you find words that people may understand better."
depts.washington.edu/respcare/public/info/Plain_Language_Thesaurus_for_Health_Communications.pdf

Manufactured by Amazon.ca
Bolton, ON

21668496R00057